Poems ANIMALS

Compiled by Brian Moses   Artwork by Kelly Waldek

WAYLAND

Titles in the series:

Poems about Food
Poems about School
Poems about Space

Editor: Sarah Doughty
Designer: Tessa Barwick

First published in 1999 by
Wayland Publishers Ltd
61 Western Road, Hove
East Sussex, BN3 1JD

find Wayland on the Internet at http://www.wayland.co.uk

© Copyright 1999 Wayland Publishers Ltd

British Library Cataloguing in Publication Data
Poems about Animals – (Wayland poetry collections)
    1. Animals – Juvenile poetry 2. Children's poetry, English
    I. Moses, Brian, 1950 –
    821.9'008'0362

ISBN 0 7502 2441 X

Printed and bound by Edições ASA, Portugal

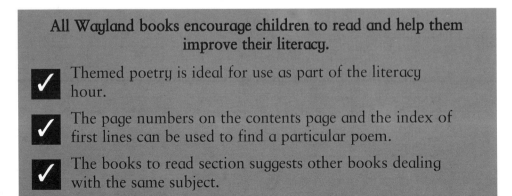

All Wayland books encourage children to read and help them improve their literacy.

✓ Themed poetry is ideal for use as part of the literacy hour.

✓ The page numbers on the contents page and the index of first lines can be used to find a particular poem.

✓ The books to read section suggests other books dealing with the same subject.

Contents

The Friendly Octopus

Eight arms for me, eight arms for me,
I'm a friendly octopus, under the sea.

 I've got

One arm to blow my nose,
One arm to wave with,
One arm to brush my teeth,
One arm to shave with,
One arm to comb my hair,
One arm to shake with,
One arm to blow a kiss,
And one to eat a cake with.

Eight arms for me, eight arms for me,
I'm a friendly octopus, under the sea.

Mike Jubb

My Pet Alligator

He crawls through the rooms
He likes to watch TV
And he almost eats everything
If he can
But if he doesn't like the food
He gets very mad
So we give him food he likes
Just to be on
The safe
side.

Thomas Bull (aged 6)

GERALDINE GIRAFFE

The
longest
ever
woolly
scarf
was
worn
by
Geraldine
Giraffe.
Around
her
neck
the
scarf
she
wound,
but
still
it
trailed
upon
the
ground.

Colin West

Granny Goat

Eat anything
will granny goat,
handkerchiefs,
the sleeve of your coat,
sandwiches,
a ten pound note.
Eat anything
will granny goat.

Granny goat
goes anywhere,
into the house
if you're not there,
follows you round,
doesn't care.
Granny goat
goes anywhere.

Granny goat
won't stay
tied up
throughout the day,
chews the rope,
wants to play.

Granny goat
won't stay
anywhere you
want her to,
she'd rather be
with you!

Brian Moses

9

Mole Shopping

The mole pokes his little snout out of doors,
He twitches his whiskers and wipes his paws.
He's tunnelled and tunnelled to reach the light
and now he's here he's got an appetite!
Mole snuffles this way and mole snuffles that,
He's hunting for worms and he likes them fat!
His larder needs filling with something that squirms,
His shopping list says   Worms
                          Worms
                          More worms

But perhaps this isn't where worms are found
So he shovels his way back underground!

Sue Cowling

Cat

My cat is black as darkest night
When no moon rides.
His eyes are green as starlit pools
And midnight tides.

But whenever the day is warm and sunny
His eyes are gold and clear as honey.
He rolls on his back and very soon
His coat is dusty with afternoon.

Ann Bonner

Cat next Door

The cat from next door
Is as quiet as a mouse;
If your front door's ajar,
Then she'll enter your house;
She will creep up the stairs
And she'll search high and low;
When she's seen all she wants,
She'll just turn tail and go.
Unless you're around
You're unlikely to know
That the cat from next door
Who's as quiet as mouse
Has enjoyed a good sniff
Through the whole of your house!

Trevor Harvey

My Rabbit

When my rabbit
is out in his run,

he digs up the ground
like a dog,

washes himself
like a squirrel,

sits on his back legs
like a kangaroo,

leaps and twirls
like an acrobat,

but

when he eats a cabbage leaf,
as is his daily habit,
he delicately nibbles it
EXACTLY like a rabbit!

June Crebbin

The Guard Dog

I'm a gruff dog, a rough dog,
I'm good in a fight.
Keep your distance
Or I might bite.

I'm a mean dog, a keen dog,
I'm quick on my paws.
Stand well back
From my vicious jaws.

I'm a proud dog, a loud dog,
Hear me growl.
One false move
And I'll make you howl.

I'm a hard dog, a guard dog,
A dog to fear.
You have been warned.
Don't come near!

John Foster

Who's seen Jip?

Jip's run away.
left home for good.
I just *knew* he would,
for earlier today
he was shouted at by dad.
    "Bad dog!
      Bad dog!
      BAD!"

    Now Jip's a stray.
What will he eat?
Where will he sleep?
I'm so sad I could weep.
Oh, doomsday, gloomsday
    my dog has gone.

Who's seen Jip?

       Anyone?

Wes Magee

17

Tarantula

She's strong,
She's scary,
She's covered in bristles.
A fighter,
A biter,
With legs like eight thistles.

A muncher,
A cruncher,
With greedy jaws gnashing.
A mawler,
A crawler ...

But I think she's SMASHING!

Clare Bevan

Beetle

Glossy black beetle
Gracefully walking
In your forest of grass.
A nest of leaves,
A crack in the wall,
You're safe at home at last!

John Cotton

Lizard

There's a lizard in my garden.
It's quiet, brown and shy.
It sunbathes on the old stone wall
and watches the giants go by.
But if we get too near
it disappears with a flick.
I love the way that lizard
is so bright eyed, neat and quick.

Penny Kent

The Tortoise

He moves so slowly,
I wonder if he can get
Wherever he wants to be.
I wonder if he has knees.
As he walks along the track
He's so small that you can't
Even see his knobbly back.
As he walks along the path
He does not even leave a mark
Like other animals in the zoo
And like people always do.

Parveen Bano Mohamed
(Africa)

Leopards

It's hard to see lions
when they lie in the grass,
or deer among trees
where they've trotted.
It's hard to see rabbits
stood in a field,
but leopards are always spotted.

Barry Buckingham

Flamingo

Flame flamingo
open your eyes.
You are the colour
of evening skies.

With feathers of fire
you're a candy-floss bird.
As your long legs step
no sound is heard.

You swing your head
and down you stretch,
from side to side,
your rosy neck.

All the colours of fire
are shining bright
as you stand by the lake
in the morning light.

Robin Mellor

Zebra

Who let them loose
   with face paints?
Who gave them pyjamas
   to wear?
Who made them look
   like newspapers?
Who striped them
   here and there?

Who designed them
   like mint humbugs?
Who painted them
   white and black?
Who thought of
   a different pattern
For each new-born
   zebra's back?

Moira Andrew

Elephants

They wear wrinkly grey coats,
big and baggy, like school uniform
on the first day of September
when mum tweaks the seams,
pulls the collar into place, says,
"Never mind, you'll grow into it!"

But elephants never do!

Moira Andrew

Do Not Disturb

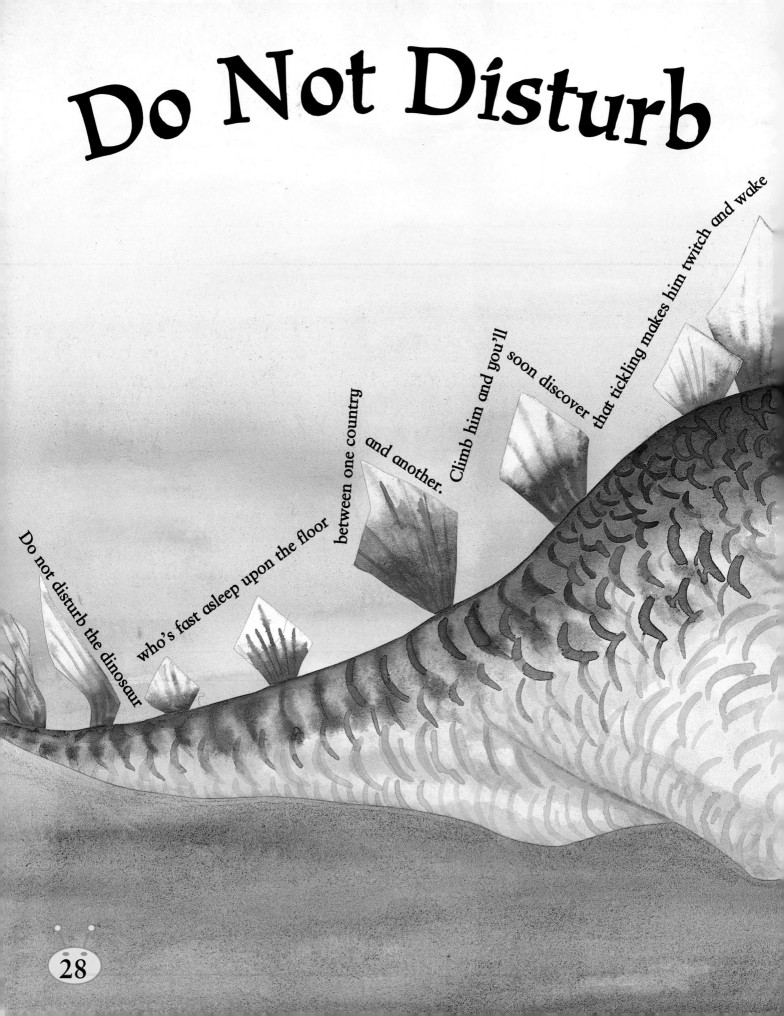

Do not disturb the dinosaur

who's fast asleep upon the floor

between one country

and another.

Climb him and you'll

soon discover

that tickling makes him twitch and wake

the Dinosaur

and scratch and cause a great earthquake and yawn a whirlwind round the world. He's better off asleep, all curled, or stretched out smiling, for a change, pretending he's a mountain range.

Gina Douthwaite

Further Information

Following on from any reading of a poem, either individually or in groups, check with the children that they have understood what the poem is about. Ask them to point out any difficult words or lines and explain these. Ask the children how they feel about the poem. Do they like it? Is there a particular section or line in the poem that they particularly enjoy?

The poems 'My Rabbit' by June Crebbin and 'Cat' by Ann Bonner are filled with lovely comparisons (similes for older children). These can be identified e.g. the rabbit who 'washes himself/like a squirrel,/ sits on his back legs/like a kangaroo, and the cat whose eyes are 'green as starlit pools/and midnight tides.' Suggest that children try to write their own ideas in the form of comparisons:

My dog is as lazy as a sloth.
His tail flaps like a flag.

My fish is like a mini torpedo,
he is golden like something King Midas touched.

Identify further comparisons in the two poems by Moira Andrew, 'Zebra' and 'Elephants'

Read 'The Guard Dog' by John Foster. This poem is written in the voice of the dog whereas many of the other poems are written from observation. Children will enjoy writing in this way. Suggest that they choose a creature and think how it might speak. Would it complain, or boast, or whine, or celebrate its life? Or would it warn as the dog does in John Foster's poem?

In 'My Pet Alligator', Thomas Bull tries to convince us that he shares his home with this creature. Children will enjoy imagining other creatures coming to stay with them – my pet hippo, rhino, piranha, dragon or monkey might well produce some imaginative stories and poems.

Mike Jubb's 'The Friendly Octopus' is a lovely piece for children to read aloud and to act out. Actions needed are quite obvious and groups of children will enjoy seeing who can come up with the liveliest performance.

'Geraldine Giraffe' by Colin West may encourage the writing of long thin wiggling poems about tall creatures while 'Do Not Disturb the Dinosaur' may inspire children to think about how they might set out shape poems of their own.

Encourage children to look for further poems about animals. These can be copied out and then illustrated.

Build up a collection of poems and let the children talk about their favourites. Let them practise reading and performing the poems.

Such activities as these will promote and reinforce the suggested work at various levels in the National Literacy Strategy.

About the Poets

Moira Andrew used to be a primary headteacher and a College of Education lecturer. She is now a full-time writer and poet in schools. Sometimes she writes about her family and her cats. "The cats don't mind, but family members sometimes do!"

Clare Bevan lives in Crowthorne, Berkshire with her husband, son and two cats. She was a teacher for years and years but she now writes stories and poems for children.

Ann Bonner lives in the West Midlands. She has been a teacher and writer for the last 35 years. She currently works as a writer in schools and a teacher of people with learning difficulties.

Barry Buckingham lives in Buckinghamshire. He was a headteacher for many years and has written numerous poems and stories for children.

Thomas Bull was born in Portsmouth in 1987. He attends St. Bede's School in Eastbourne and enjoys sport and playing his guitar.

John Cotton lives with his dog Rosie in Berkhamstead. He meets lots of young people on the Pearse House Creative Writing courses that he tutors in Saffron Walden. His book *The Poetry File* (Macmillan) is widely used in schools.

Sue Cowling has moved a number of times but now lives in the Midlands. She writes a lot of animal poems and gets some of her ideas while out walking her dog Toffee.

June Crebbin lives in Birstall, Leicestershire with her husband and her rabbit. She was a primary school teacher in England and the USA before taking early retirement in order to concentrate on writing. She is the author of a number of books.

Gina Douthwaite lives high on the Yorkshire Wolds where she writes poetry and stories for children. She also runs Poetry Parties in schools and a collection of shape poetry, *Picture a Poem* was published by Hutchinson in 1994.

John Foster taught English for over twenty years. He has edited numerous collections of poetry for children and has had eight books of his own poetry published. He lives in Oxfordshire and regularly visits schools and libraries to perform his poems.

Trevor Harvey claims to be a descendant of St. George, although he has never fought any dragons. He was a principal lecturer at the University of Brighton and now pretends to spend all his time writing stories, poems and plays.

Mike Jubb lives in Fareham, Hampshire with his two children and three pet rats. He used to be a teacher but now earns his living as a writer visiting schools. His poems are widely anthologised and a picture book *Splosh!* is published by Scholastic.

Penny Kent was born in Surrey and at present lives in a little farming village in Bavaria with her husband, son and daughter. She has had poems published in a variety of children's books.

Wes Magee was born in Greenock, Scotland and now lives in North Yorkshire. He is a former headteacher and has been a full time author since 1989. His most recent book is *The Phantom's Fang-tastic Show* (OUP).

Robin Mellor lives in Kent with his wife, Ann. He used to be a headteacher but now works full-time as a writer. His poems appear in many anthologies and a story book *Mr Stofflees and the Painted Tiger* is published by OUP.

Brian Moses lives on the coast in Sussex with his wife and two daughters. He writes and edits books for children and travels the country performing his poems. His latest anthology *The Worst Class in School* is published by Wayland.

Colin West was born in Essex and left school at the earliest opportunity to study art. His first book was a collection of his nonsense verse published in 1976. Since then he has produced many picture books, story books and more poetry books.

Permissions

The compiler and publisher would like to thank the authors for allowing their poems to appear in this anthology. While every attempt has been made to gain permissions and provide an up-to-date biography, in some cases this has not been possible and we apologise for any omissions.

Books to Read

Amazing Animal Alphabet with Fantastic Flaps written by Richard Edwards, illustrated by Sue Hendra (OUP). A lovely book with a riddle for each letter of the alphabet and flaps which reveal the hidden creatures.

Animal Stories by Dick King-Smith (Puffin). These are short stories along with extracts from two of the author's most popular books *The Sheep-Pig* and *The Hodgeheg*. There are many other books by this author to suit all ages and abilities.

Hairy Maclary from Donaldson's Dairy by Lynley Dodd (Puffin). Engaging rhyming text and delightful pictures combine here. Meet such characters as Hercules Morse Bottomley Potts and Scarface Claw. Check out the other titles in this series too.

Dinosaur Roar! by Paul and Henrietta Stickland (Ragged Bears & Puffin). A whole range of wonderful dinosaurs are featured here along with a rhyme that children will enjoy learning by heart.

Sheltie the Shetland Pony by Peter Clover (Puffin). First of a series of books about Sheltie which will get newly independent readers hooked on reading.

Gorilla by Anthony Browne (Walker Books). Striking and witty illustrations in a story of a lonely girl and a friendly gorilla. A classic.

Turtle Bay by Saviour Pirotta, illustrated by Nilesh Mistry (Frances Lincoln). A story to make children think about wild animals and how we treat them.

Animal Poems compiled by Jennifer Curry (Hippo Books). Read about the big-bottomed hippo and the worm who went to Wembley!

Picture acknowledgements Bruce Coleman 15 (Jane Burton), 20 (George McCarthy), 24/25 (Luiz Claudio Margio).

Author permissions: 'My Pet Alligator' by Thomas Bull from *Wundercrump Poetry*, 1994; 'Granny Goat' by Brian Moses from *Twinkle, Twinkle Chocolate Bar* (OUP); 'Cat' by Ann Bonner from *Stories for Bedtime* (Collins, 1995); 'My Rabbit' by June Crebbin from *The Jungle Sale* (Viking Kestrel, 1994); 'The Guard Dog' by John Foster © 1999; 'Zebra' by Moira Andrew from *The Wider World* (Riverpoint Publishing, 1998); 'Do not Disturb the Dinosaur' from *Picture a Poem* (Hutchinson, 1994) by Gina Douthwaite © 1994.

Index of First Lines